Tanya Stone

Eve

Published by: Stone Inc.

Text Design by: Tanya Stone

Cover Design by: Bee & Stone

ISBN-10: 1-7333344-1-6

ISBN-13: 978-1-7333344-1-9

Distributed by: Stone Inc.

For my honeybee:
You make all things possible, my muse,
my new beginning, my split-apart, and my every
reason why. I choose you each and every day.
Thank you for believing in me. Eternally - T

EVE

TANYA STONE

She’s not me
and I know somedays
you thank the gods she’s not
and other days
you curse ever laying eyes on me
and even more
one day
you’ll remember everything we denied
because it happened
we were there
and we were real
if just for a moment
but for now
we are simply black ink
on white paper
this is where we live
flowing from my pen
not me and memory.

/ink and memory/

I want you to know
I've hidden love notes all over your life
and I hope you still find them
at exactly the moments when I still
hide
from the places that remind me of us.
What I mean is
I want you to know you are loved
for that shimmy you do when you dance
through my head
in our bedroom
that night we stayed up until the sun
lipsyncing the songs that would play at our wedding.
I flowed like honey in your hands
because honey you are my bee
stinging me in the morning with kisses
and flying away with slammed doors.
Opening
my eyes to the lifetimes between us
that promises can't cross
out
from the lines on my face
and the hurt that we've said.
I want you to know
every time you said I wasn't enough
I believed you.
I tattooed all that shame across my chest
backward
so when I wash myself clean and stand in the mirror
I don't forget who I really am.

I want you to know
I love you
and I'm doing that thing
where I practice loving myself.
I'm up to a few moments each day
that ticks by wondering
if you look at the sky
finding shapes in the clouds
painted on my toes
on the island of our bed
that I dared to dream
would keep us from drowning.
I want you to know
when I begged you to stay
I meant it
stay exactly how you are
perfect
and I imagine how hard it was to love me
because I only think I can be loved when I am perfect
which only adds to my imperfection
so I'm guaranteed
to come back each life
to find you again.

/honeybee/

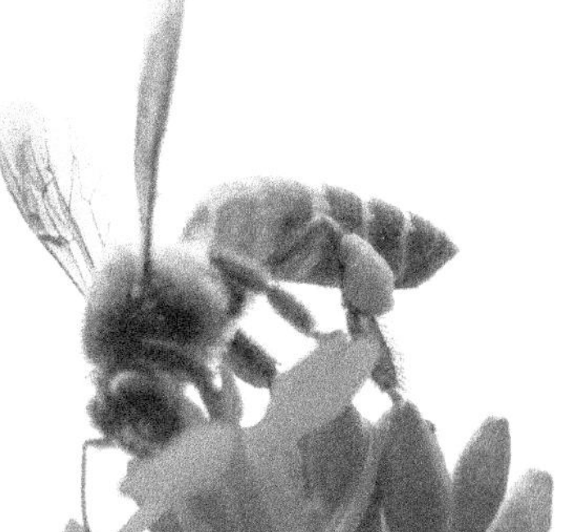

I have searched my whole life
for my place
amongst the strange and sea
art and the obscure
fool-heartedly pining
longitude and latitude
when truth is
all I ever dreamed
of living in was
you

/search/

There's a wad of twenties
stuffed in old black pantyhose
in Aunt Delores's sock drawer,
a five gallon jug of quarters
almost full in my friend's closet,
airline miles for a someday escape
promises for tomorrowland
and rainy day safety nets
when there's blackness between wins.
Life is like that
I imagine pillars
of what some might say is happiness
and valleys between
gaps filled with space
working towards the next one
or hanging on to threads of a twisted rope
worrying if this is the time I fall
down
further than you'll reach to lift me back up,
so I keep mine in my back pocket
the ace of spades.

I've laid it down a time or two
more than I will ever tell
a soul
both ashamed and enamored
by my good luck charm
running my fingers over scuffed edges
shuffled into this deck of a life
it soothes me
mine alone to play
anytime I choose
to end the game.

/rainy day suicide/

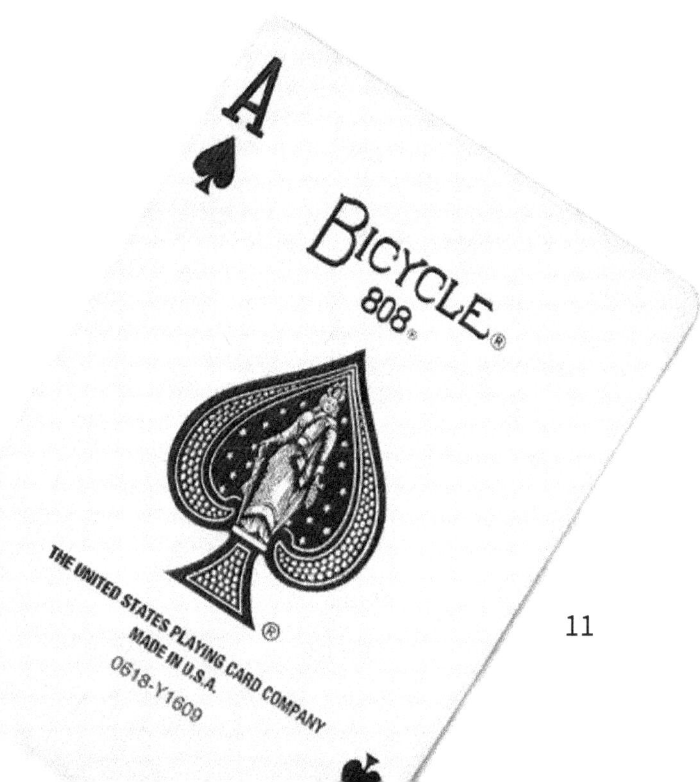

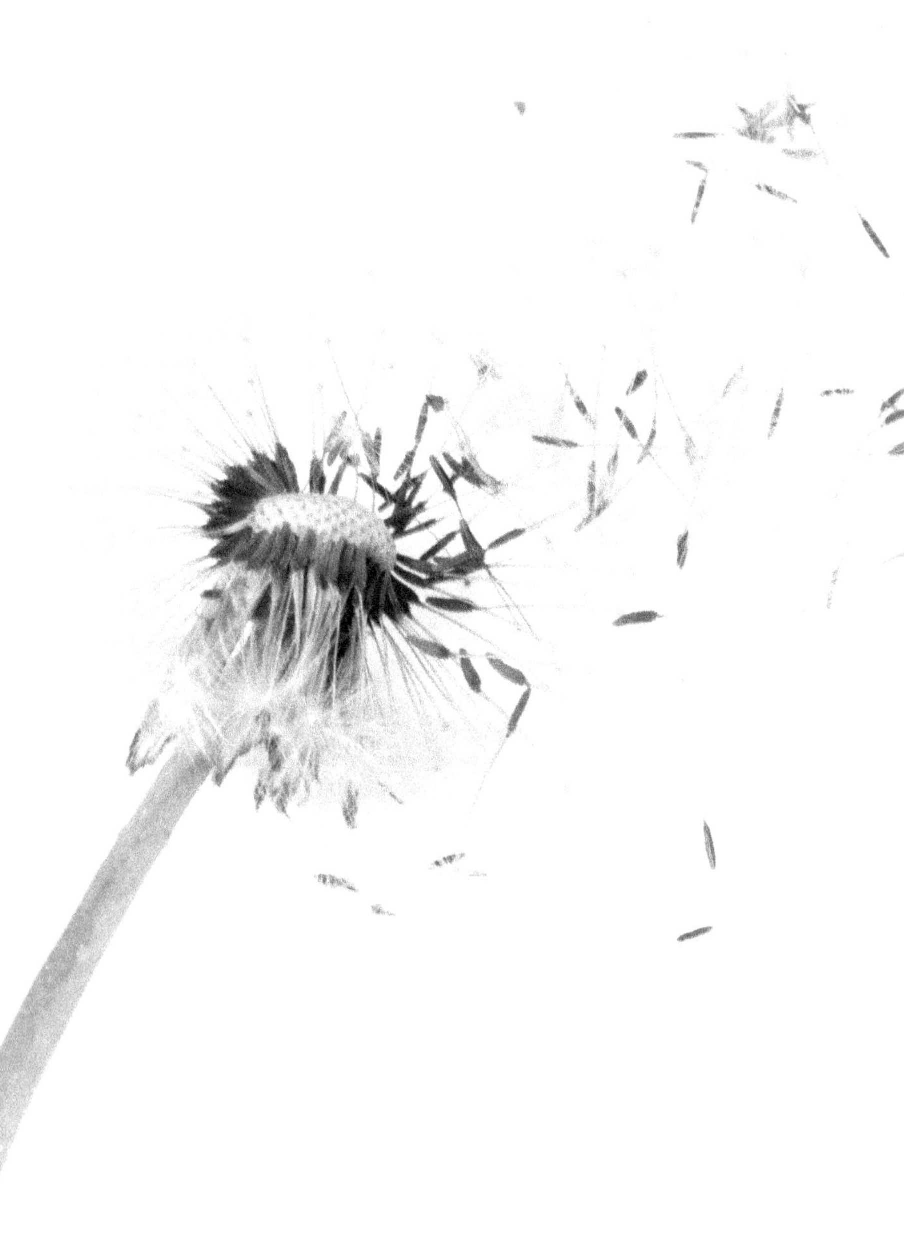

Does she watch you sleeping
In the early morning?
Does she laugh at all your randomness?
Does she reach for you in the middle of the night?
Does she love Cash, Elvis and the Blues like we do?
Does she tell you
you are the most beautiful woman alive?
Everyday?
Because you are.
Does she drive with you until you're lost?
And then photograph you in the last light of sun?
Does she dance with you at rest stops?
Does she love you like I did?
Like I do?
Well, does she?
Then why not me?

/why not/

You know who it is that wins?
Those women that get carried off
into the sunset
like a goddamn Disney movie,
it's the women who listen.
Stay with me now
because every bone in my feminist body
tells me to lay across the tracks
of this thought train
but there's something there.
The women and men who win
are the ones who don't need to win
the ones who don't need to be right
and then they end up winning by default.
Is it because they fake a smile through that bullshit
or maybe they don't see it as shit
and maybe it's not shit at all
but the human-ness of another human
and they just stay silently nodding
stifling sharpe tongues
or maybe they're not biting their tongues
or sighing and rolling their eyes
because maybe they don't know the truth

or maybe there isn't any truth to know at all.
Maybe in the times that something is
so absofuckinglutely true
like the sky is blue
it's so absurd to even argue
so they don't
and they let their person believe the sky is fuchsia
or hear them say
"honey, look at the beautiful, clear chartreuse sky"
and simply sigh and think
"Wow you're so magic baby
because you see things differently than I do."
while looking at the clear, blue sky
because maybe they don't care about the sky at all
and it's more important to have love
and be loved
than to be right.
Maybe that's who makes it in life
the couple holding hands
admiring the clear, chartreuse sky together.

/the clear chartreuse sky/

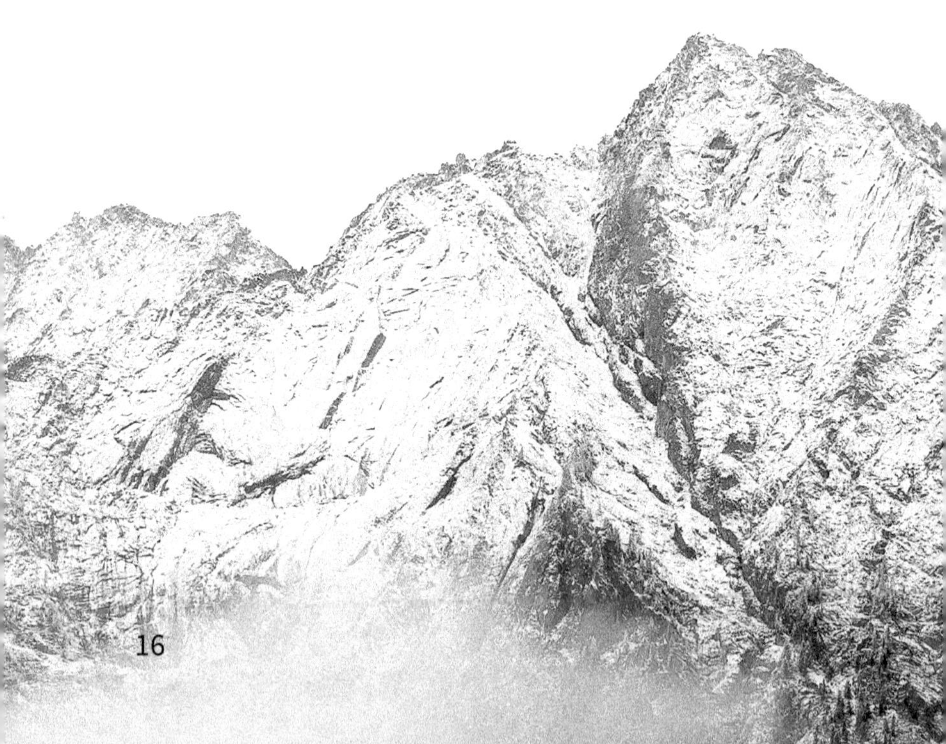

If I could
I would tie your hands
to our bravest memory
sing you our song
as I'm picking you
out of my smile
because even these words
belong to you
I love you the same way
I climbed a mountain the first time
wanting to quit
wondering why I bother to do it
reveling at the beauty of it all
because I can
I want to do
what no one has dared to do
trust you.

/if only/

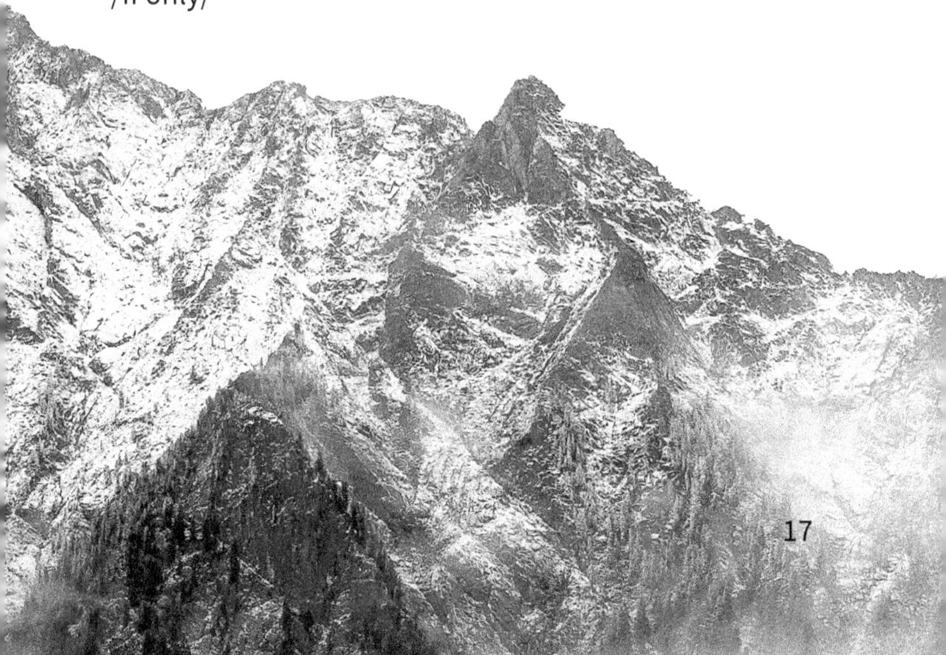

I’ve had such a lovely time this life
I shall surely do it again
except next go round
I will pay less attention to the rules
after all, stability is the calling card
of the mundane and unimaginative
while freedom and dance
belong to the next me
dangerous and daring
alight with folly and afterlife
and if there are such things as sin
then I shall try them on for truth.

/reincarnation/

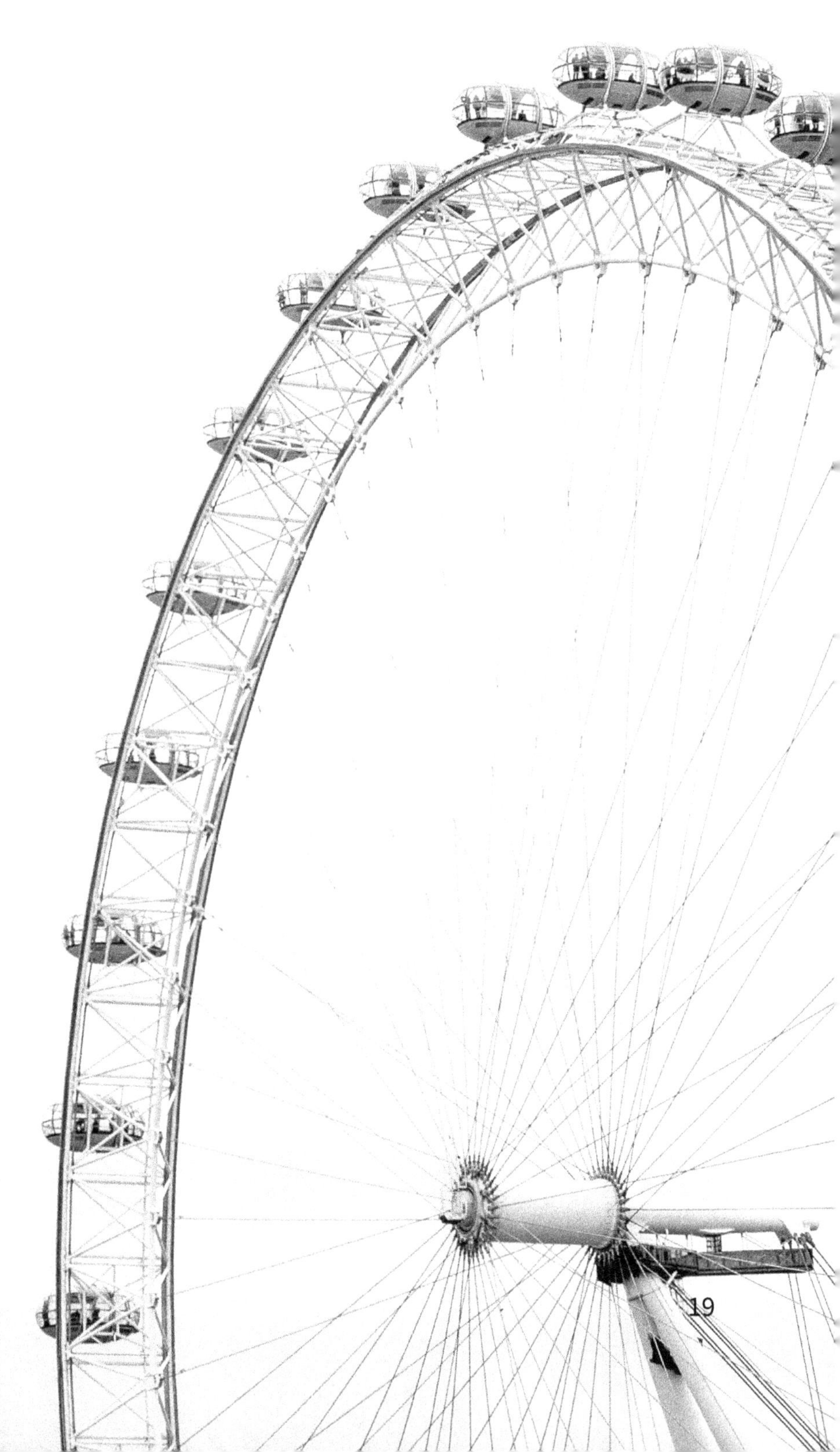

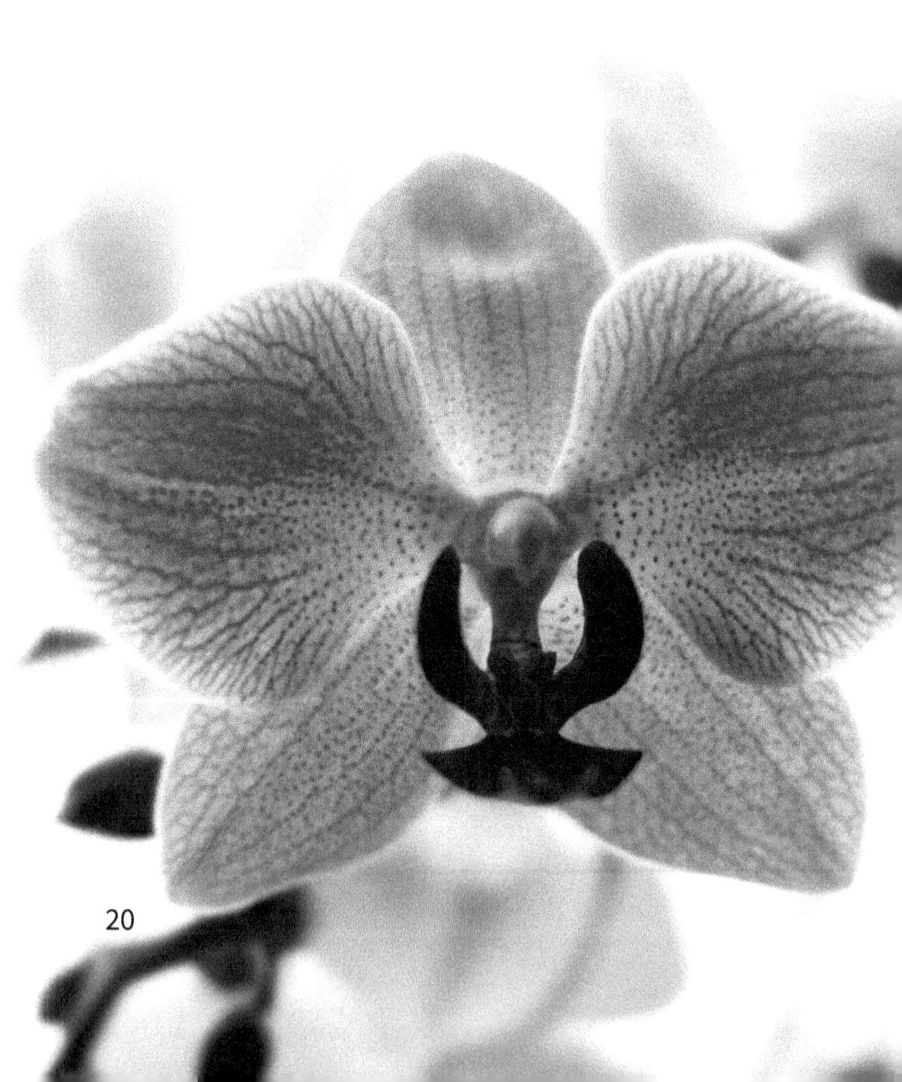

In all the lifetimes of eternity
there will never be anything
more beautiful than our bodies
entwined last night
breathing life into sunken chests
my mating cries
there's a dance or two
in these old bones still.

/the dance/

Dig beneath the shallow and uncover
gnarled and determinedly hellhound limbs
stretching, reaching
for further destinations
than tender emerald arms
rising from the dark
and dancing with storm clouds
I am contracting beauty
waving banners of self-love
to the sun and rain
receiving both to shower
the succulent song spread
in love's sweet blossom dying to wilt
and rise again.

/roots/

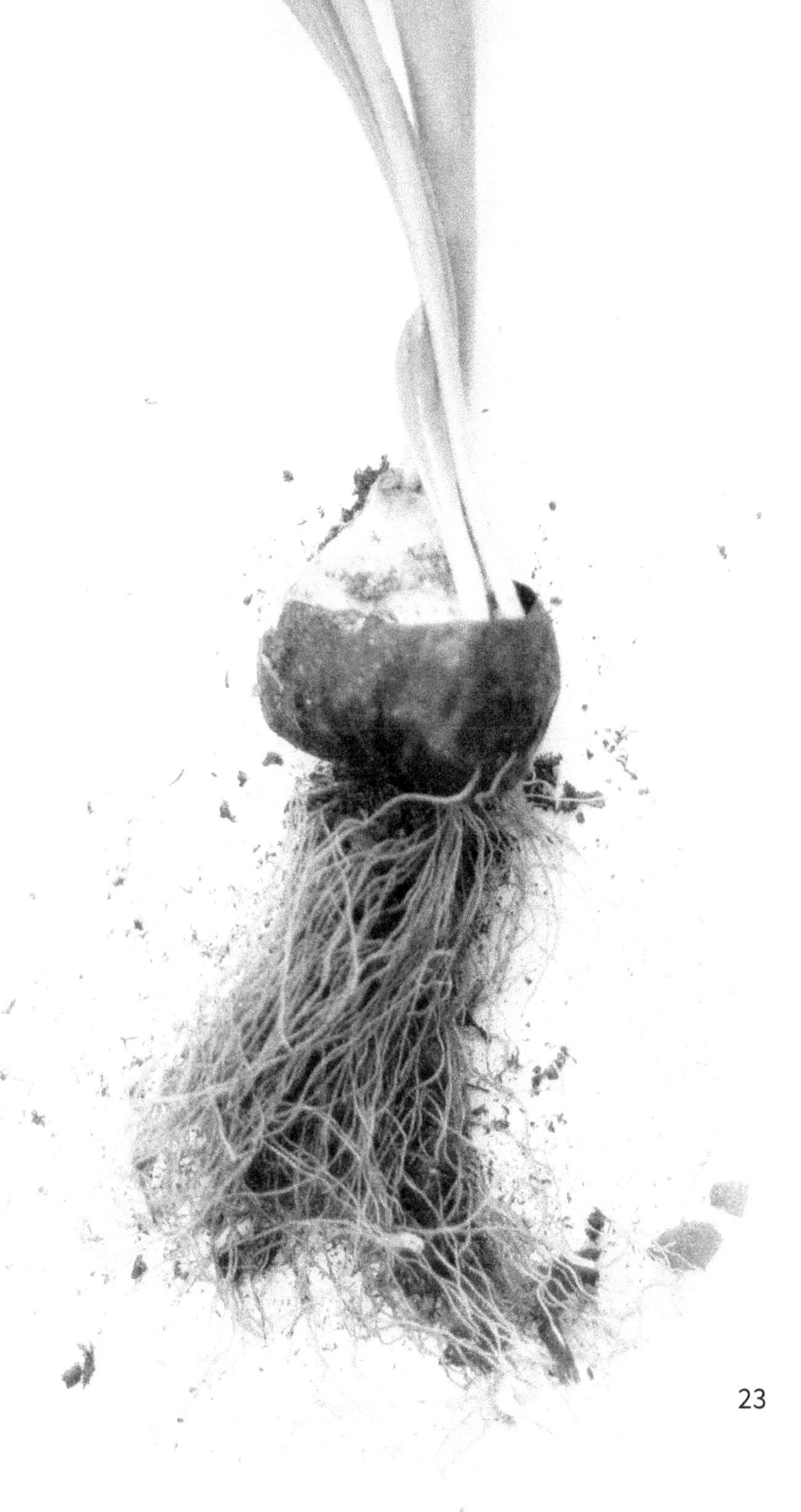

Dreams of a soft death
an escape from this hard life
that made me into something else
between a pre-existing condition
and predisposition
of too much for too long.
I pine for the strength
to puff up instead of shrink
from your anger and distaste.
Your anger is palpable
and I dream of the days
when I loved myself for how I once was
and I'm thinking there must be a way to go back
or forget the awe, the desire, the bliss of you
because you knock the wind out of my sails
frought with timid eggshell footsteps
and leave bite marks on my heart
that I photoshop out of family pictures of us.

/teeth/

It's Friday afternoon pour me a celebratory
Drink
and I can't remember the last time you just stared
into my eyes for the sake of seeing me
Drink
how it hurts to feel you slipping away from me
within arm's reach
Drink
I'm turning apathetic to other's stories
of serving time, serving our country,
or coffee in a greasy diner,
as long as I'm served another
Drink
because nothing I do is good enough
or good at all anymore
Drink
I'm slowly learning to be quiet
when the fighting starts
I just need to cool off
a little time to sit and
Drink
and it's hard to hear anything
but the screaming silence
of your back to me at night
Drink
I'll find a way out of this mess, I swear
because I love you like a promise
I intend to keep right after this
Drink
and you say things would be different

if we didn’t get so angry when we
Drink
but those sweet words and apologies
are empty and hollow after we
Drink
while smiling at messages on your phone
silently cautious, not hearing me speak
Drink
we’re strangers who imagined
we couldn’t live without each other
Drink
I’ve seen it in movies
grey-haired lovers who conquered time
Drink
I imagine that would have been us
before we fell into the
Drink
and that stings
so the more it hurts
the more I
Drink
until the pain
turns to numbness obliterated out by the
Drink
I wonder, baby
would you blame me
for the mess of us
or would you blame the
Drink

/drink/

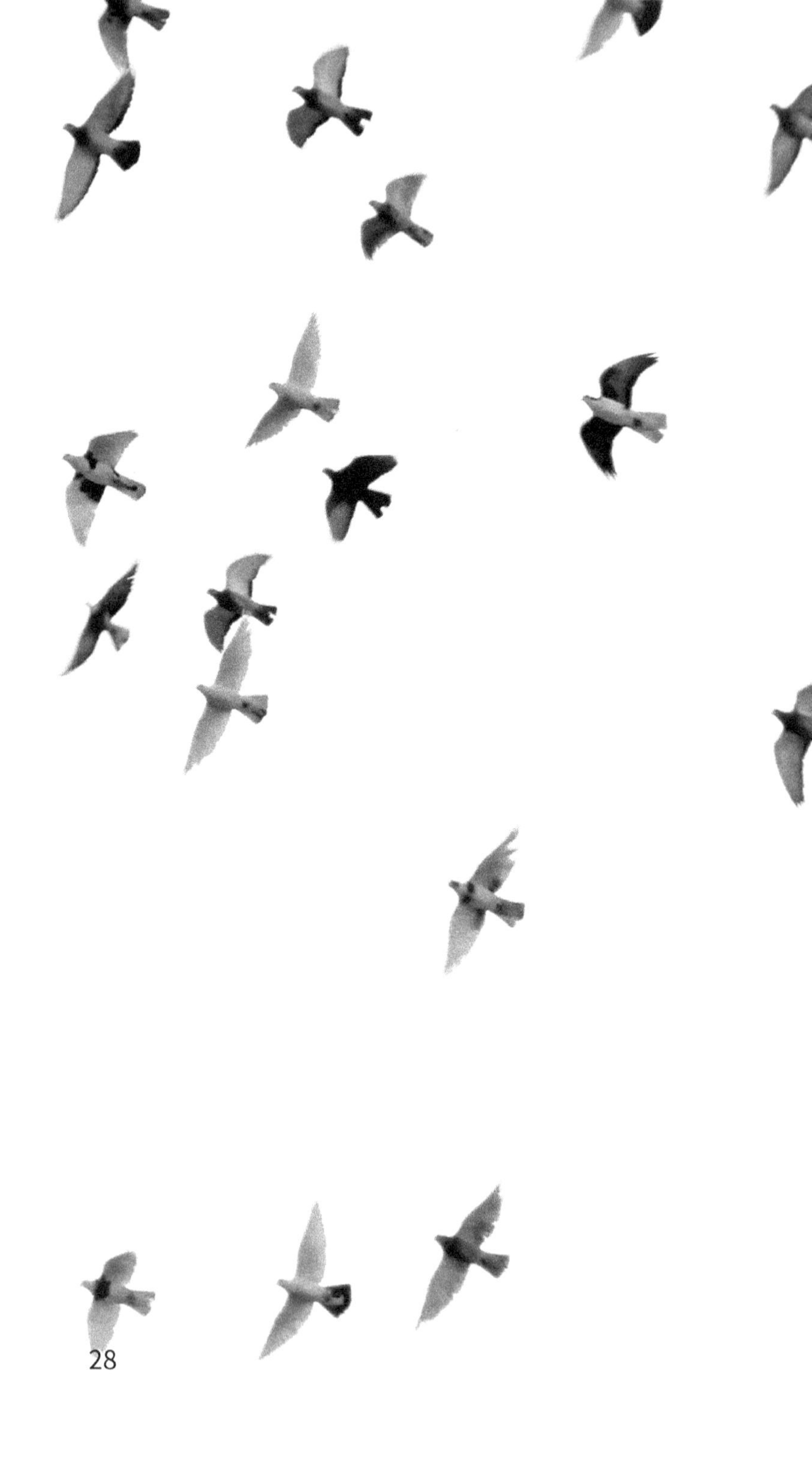

If we fly hard enough
will we get to the sun
because I've been in the dark for weeks
and you're my guiding light
I'm losing sight of the fire
while I burn life down around me
I pray we are phoenix
to rise out of the ash I've made.

/phoenix/

I think my favorite You is the one I leave
because there is this longing for each other
that we don't have day to day
the "I need you" we forget to say
in casual conversations of have-to's.
There's this reach I do
across each mile I drive
away from home
and it's those short trips
too far from you
that remind me
you are who I will always return to.
I am a child counting down to Christmas
unwrapping your body with mine
my sinew knows not to soften
until I return
shoulders hunched towards ears
hands tight, jaw clenched, breath shallow
and I see our exit on the highway
those butterflies take flight
thumping in my chest
like the girl in the vintage dress with flowers
for the girl wearing the bowtie on a first date
my stomach dips as I turn onto our street
and I cannot contain my smile.
Before you, my life was made of plans of running
far away and the spaces in between leaving
but with you, my days are filled with home
and the returning to you.

/on going away/

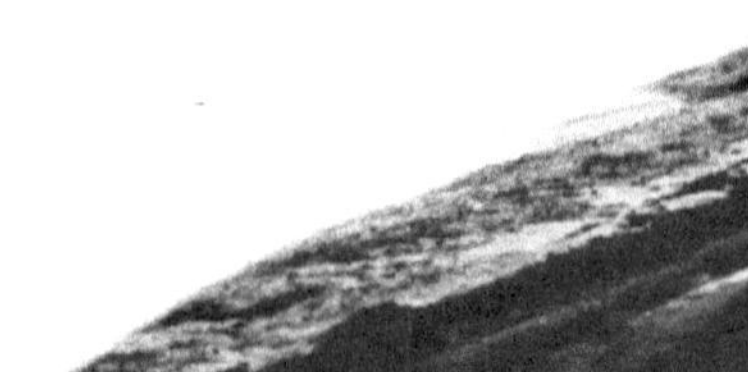

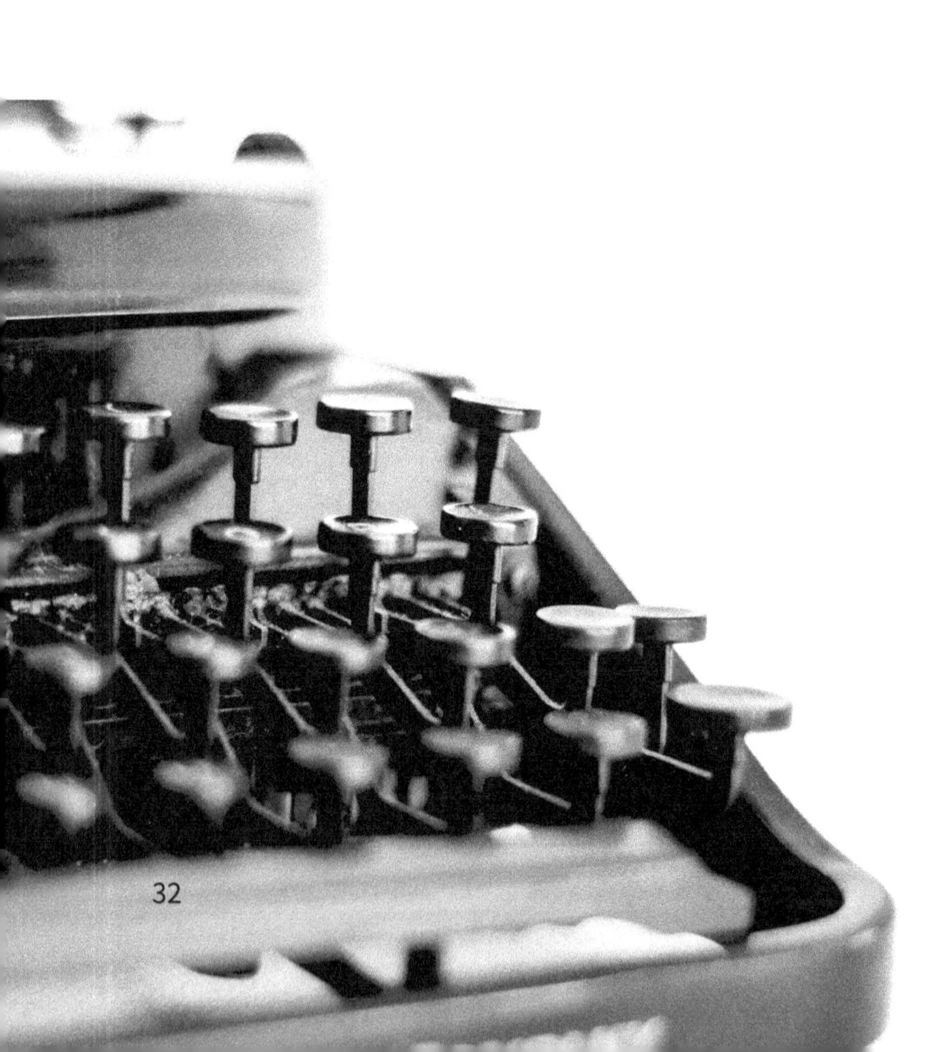

I can try as I might
to write you all the ways
I love you
or wish I'd loved you
right
down to the simplest
detail of your sigh in sleep
but the truth is
you are not the words
you are all the spaces in between them
the magic that conjures
my genius to light
and that
cannot be written.

/right/

She had no footing
only floated
driftwood to driftwood
lost at sea
uncaring
where the current
would take her
as long as she stayed
afloat.

/driftwood/

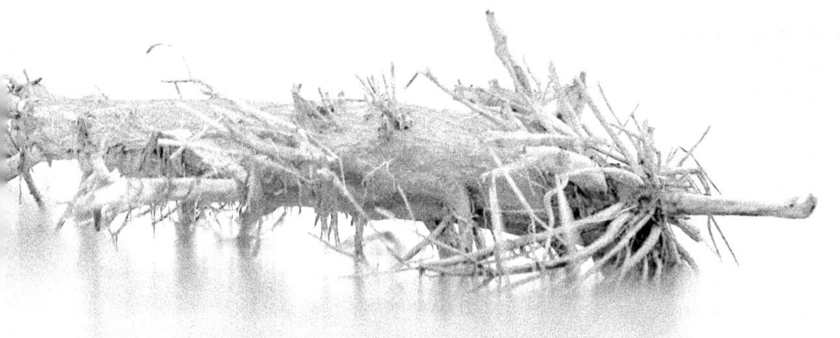

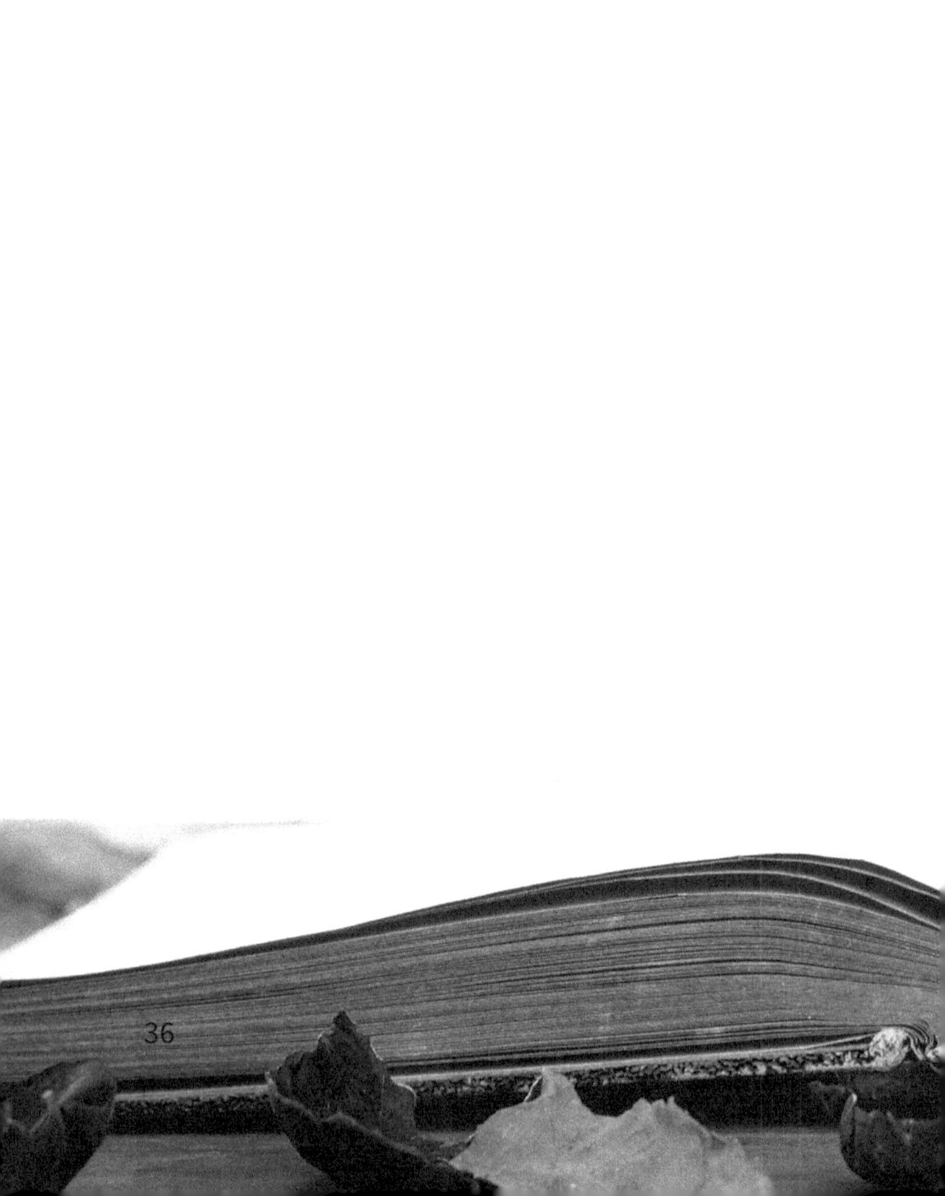

When I met you
I understood all the colors
I'd read about in storybooks
of far away places
your name on my tongue
the falling of snowflakes
of the first snowfall
of winter.

/falling/

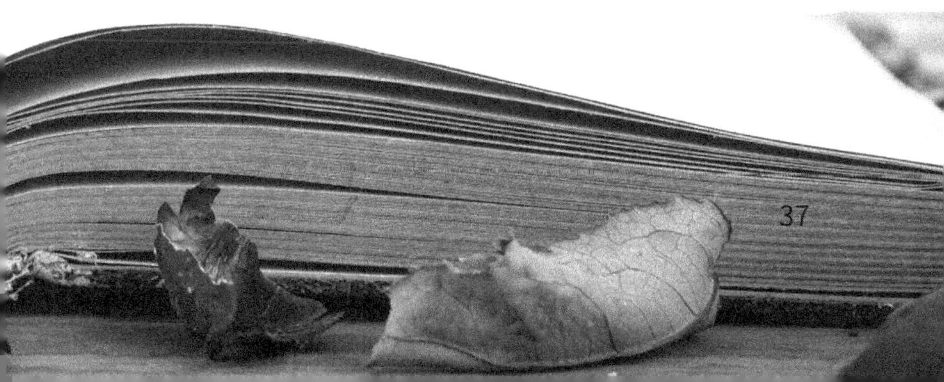

She said I make her feel small
I suppose that's true
for when I feel small
I climb the highest branch
and trample down upon her
crushing her beneath my weight
lest she forget
I am heavier than she.

/gravity/

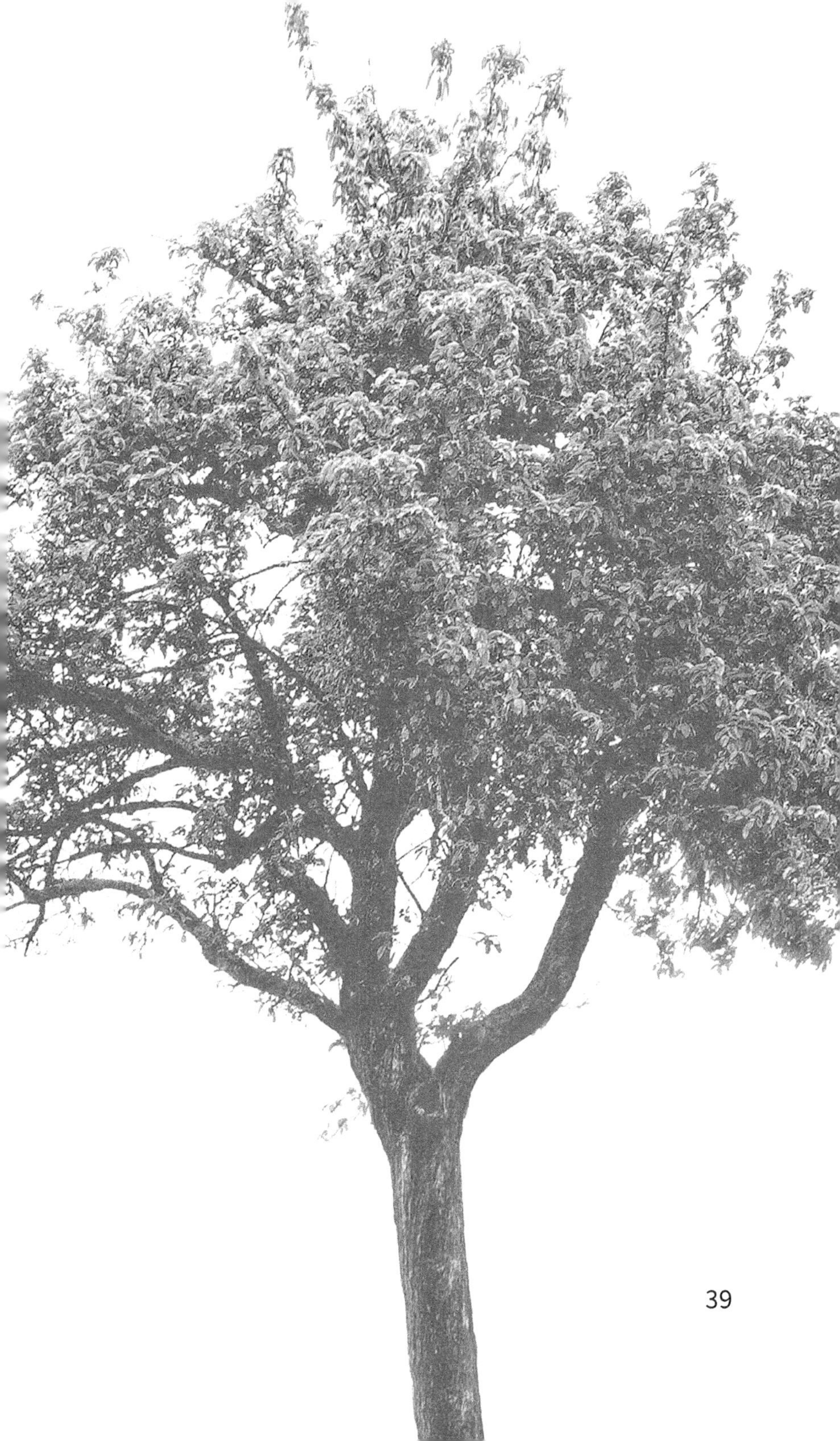

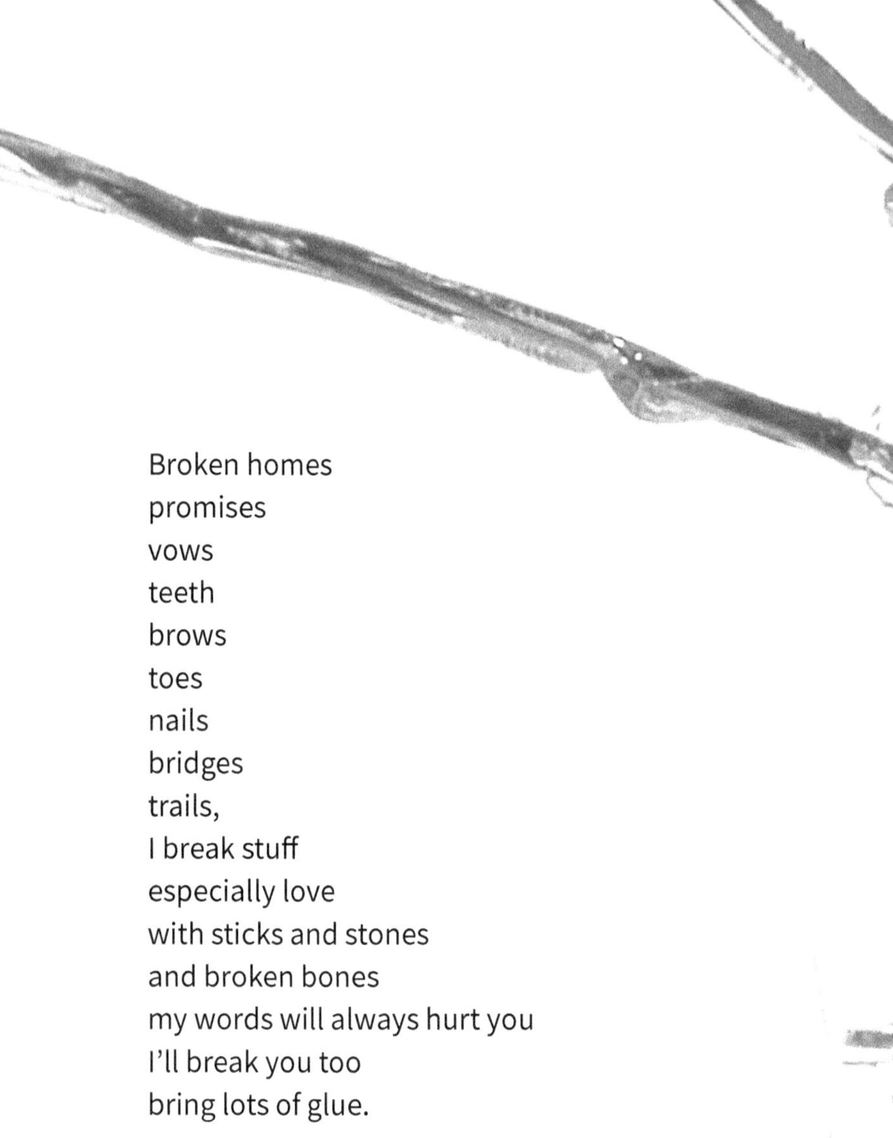

Broken homes
promises
vows
teeth
brows
toes
nails
bridges
trails,
I break stuff
especially love
with sticks and stones
and broken bones
my words will always hurt you
I'll break you too
bring lots of glue.

/broken things/

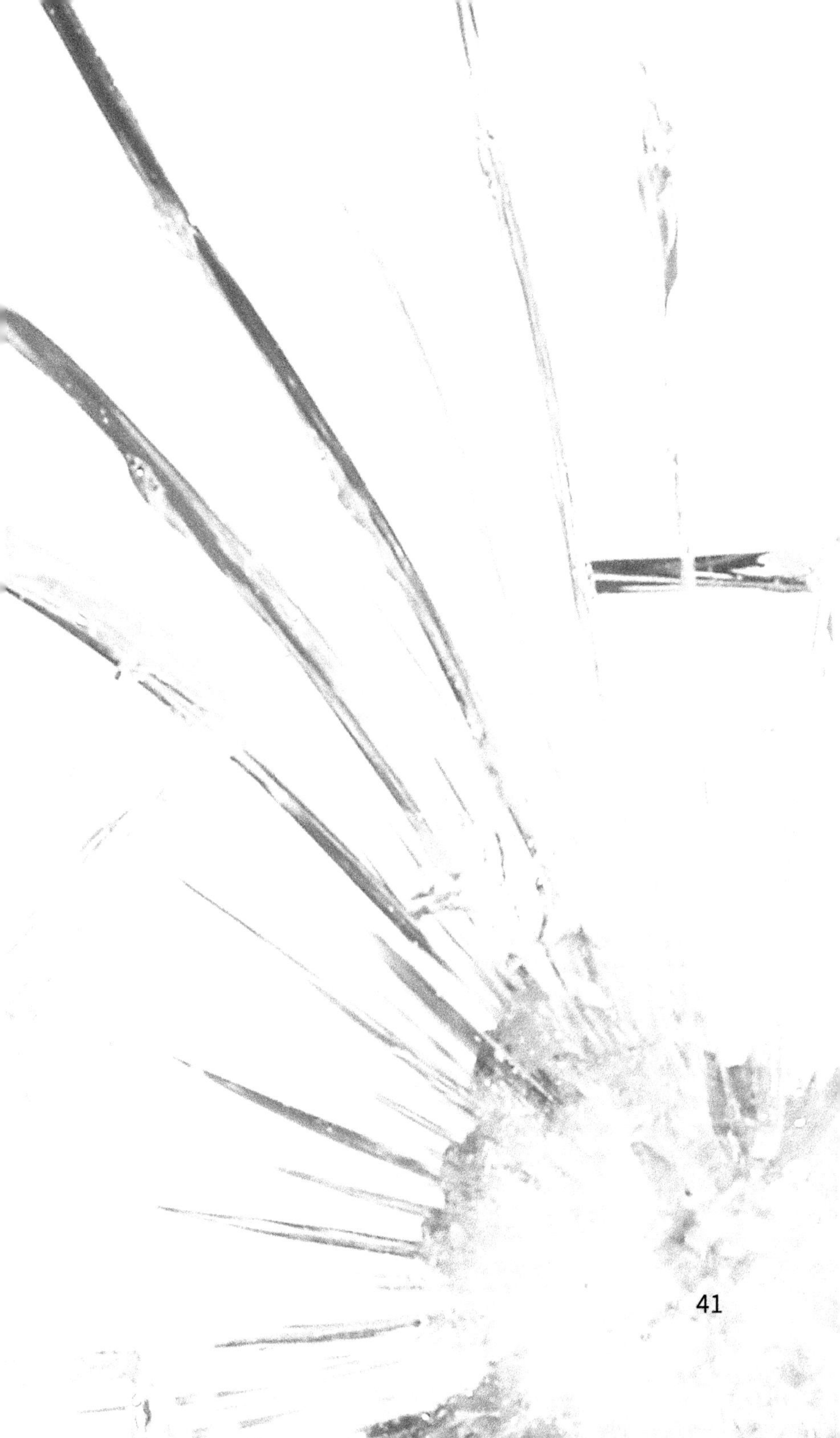

Lovers and lessons sent to me
like tides and storms
until I am smooth
like an ocean stone
worn
tumbled
etched
smooth
concentrated
turned
spit out
sucked back in
skipped along the surface
rounded
polished
shaped
eroded
formed
etched
sinking to resurface
until I am a sand
between your toes.

/ocean stone/

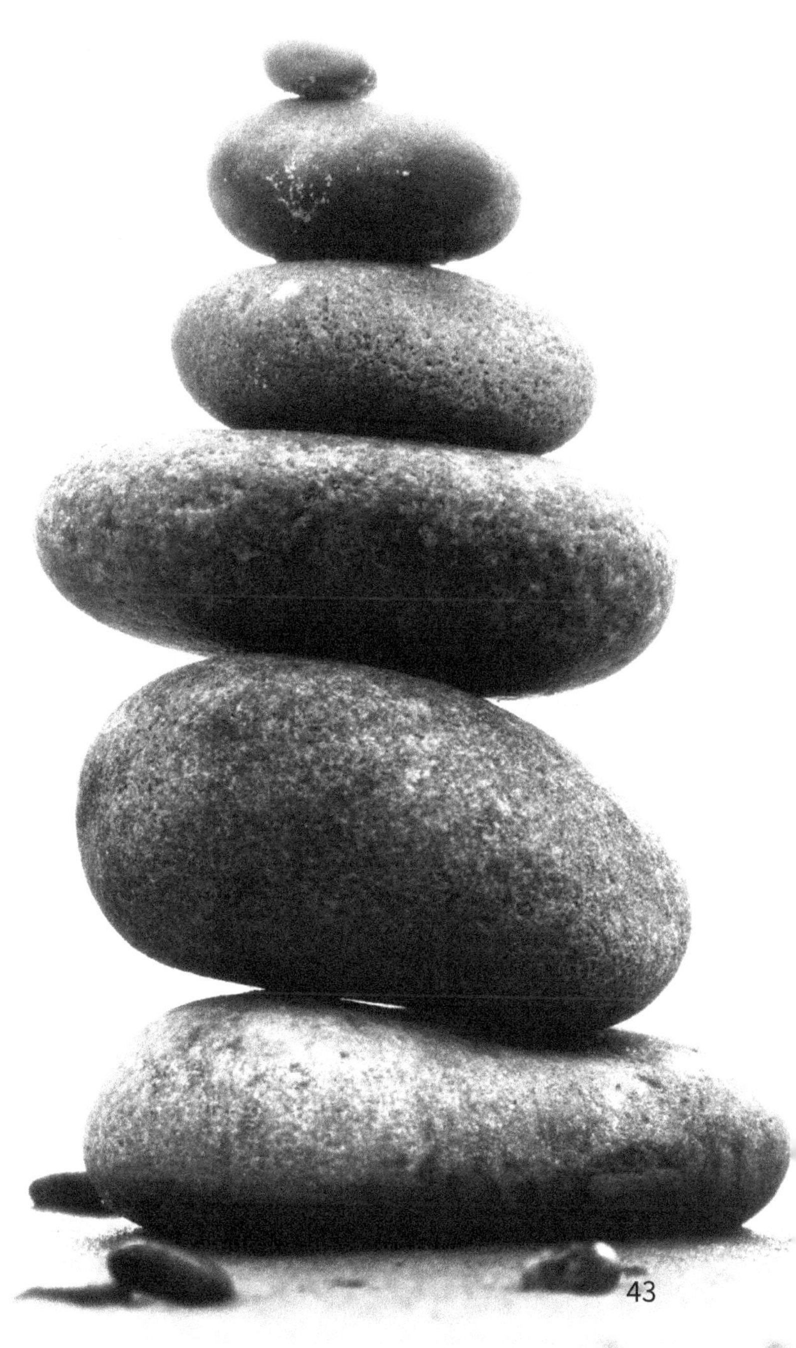

Maybe Eve was framed
and women have been carrying fictional shame
that scarlet letter burden one-way hypocrisy
since the dawn of existence,

Maybe Eve was the foreshadowed activist
to Gloria Steinem and Audre Lorde
declaring our right of choice
rather than the acceptance of
the trojan horse gift of manmade rule,

Maybe Eve planted seeds of rebellion
of defiant echoes in our wombs
the ripple effect Roe vs Wade
the penning of Our Bodies Ourselves
the precursor for Saudi women demanding to drive,

Maybe Eve marched out of that garden
in protest of the patriarch
leading the way for Alice Paul and Lucy Burn
to march for women's right to vote
and for Catherine Brewer to become
the first woman to get a college degree,

Maybe Eve was a wayseer
of broader horizons of invention
than the paternal greenhouse
creating the space for feminine innovation
of Marie Curie's two Nobel peace prizes
for medical miracles
and Ada Lovelace's mathematic foundations
of programming.

Maybe Eve is to be revered
for her courage to question authority
like Rosa Parks refused to give up her seat
And Emmeline Pankhurst's hunger strike
in the face of female suffrage,

Maybe Eve was just plain hungry
and tired of being told
what she could and could not do
with her own body
by some white man
on a self-proclamed throne of power,

Maybe Eve is in me
and maybe Eve is you
and she's our daughters
and our sisters
reminding us that
we've been shamed
and held small too long
and it's the time to celebrate
the eve of our creation.

/eve/

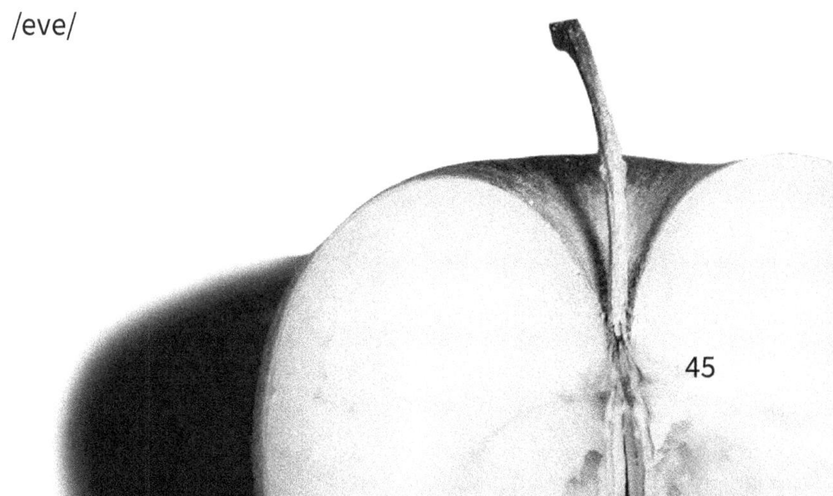

At thirteen when we recorded ourselves
saying society makes us spies
how we lost and found each other
physically and within each other
my vault
keeper of secrets and dreams
acapela shower singer
with made up song lyrics
best friend
midnight rescues and escape plans
running away from home
to our mothers to save them
from what we ran away from
bonded over masks we wore
of perfect exteriors
and broken homes
you were the only one
who knew I was a siren
and reminded me
so many years later
what I'd forgotten.

/siren/

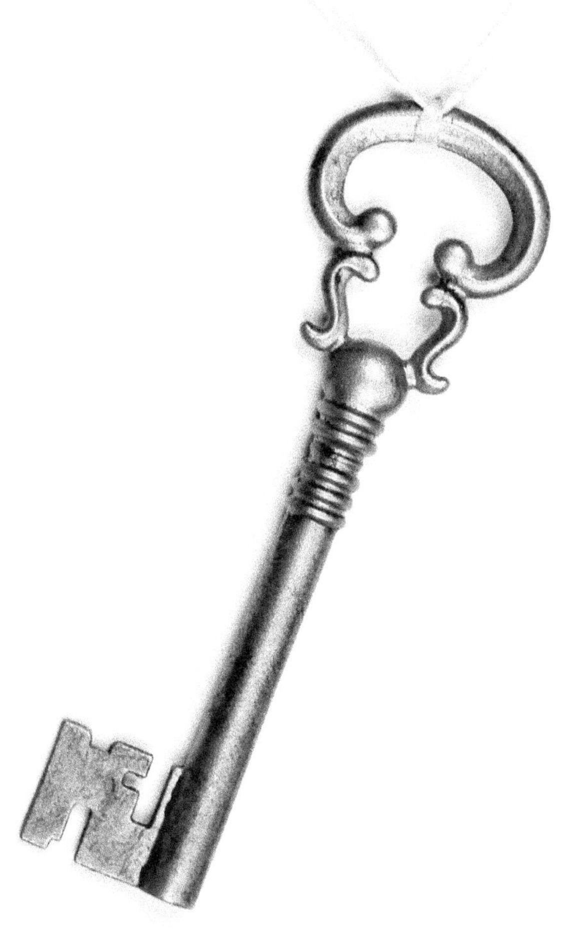

In a parallel universe
I ask your name
introduce myself
we smile at each other
shyly
having watched
pretending not to notice
the other watching
studying your every curve
the angels of your frame
the silhouette of your face
the way your head bows
when you catch me staring,
I don't look away
daring you to look back.

In a parallel universe
we go for coffee
make awkward conversation
knowing there will be a date
and a second
and a third.

In a parallel universe
we fall in love
you are tender and kind
we make love whenever it rains.

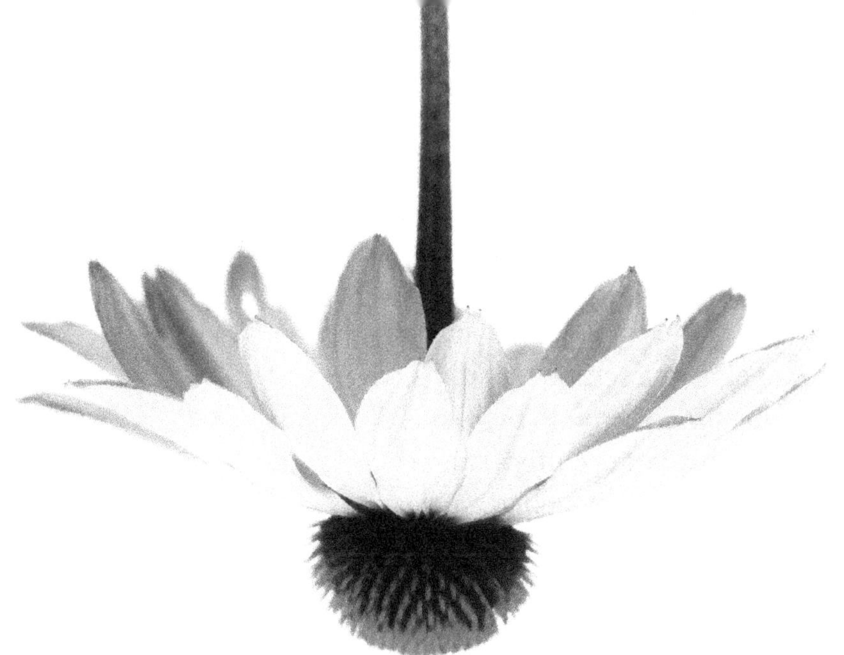

In a parallel universe
we are happy
we are together
we are one.

In this one
I was too afraid.

/parallel me/

Sometimes I imagine myself
a web intricately woven
each night with gossamer silk
and right before sleep snatches me away
the perfect geometry of my mind is clear
against the setting sun of the day
then forgotten with the winds of dreams
blown apart, a pattern snared
shuffling the meaning to my being
so that the morning dew lays ruin
to the last tendrils of what I knew of truth.
Other times, I am orderly
stacked floors of a skyscraper
the lobby decorated with pleasantries
at the checkout counter
where I read your name tag
and you call me ma'am
never imagining to take the elevator
to the subgenius floor
for fear I'll trap you inside.
On occasion, I catch sight of me
in the seemingly chaotic ruffles
of the Mexican girls' undercoats
endless lines of undulating ruffles
dipping and peeking
in a whirling hypnotic merry-go-round
mesmerizing pretenatural billows
begging impossible touch
but halting on your fingertips
a spell broken in mid song.

Occasionally I spy myself in catchlights
of wave crests during the golden hours
a pale wash of pinks and orange
piggybacking forming crests
or in the sunbeams
piercing Spanish moss
particle highways and prisms
dancing on walls
bouncing through old bottles
on window sills
in a nameless colonial town.
And that is what it's been like
to remember who I am
or was, or will be.
Momentary glimpses of magic
a brief knowing
from the corner of my eye
vanishing so quickly as shown
forgotten in the mundane
waking and shuffling
of the in-betweens
until the next showing.

/glimpses of myself/

I promise you, beautiful soul
you won't waste a rainy afternoon
unloved, alone and lonely
without love's sweet caress
tangled in limbs
under warm cotton sheets
as the raindrops keep time
with the current
running between us
applauding your surrender.

/rainy days/

Isn't it funny how we celebrate weight
knowing exactly how much matter
we formed on our entrance of life.
7 pounds, 8 ounces.
Yet nobody recalls your substance on exit
eulogizing the mass of curated existence
multiplying, dividing and dying.
No one says look how far she's come
from her birth weight to today
and what a beautiful array of scars and stories
she wore through the seasonal changes.
And wouldn't it be a greater truth
if we told our ages by season or phase
rather than man's measured trips around the sun
like a silhouetted mountain lined in tree trunks
finer hair of shed leaves on a wisened scalp
with weathered skin to endure the cold
of middle age entering winter's celebration.

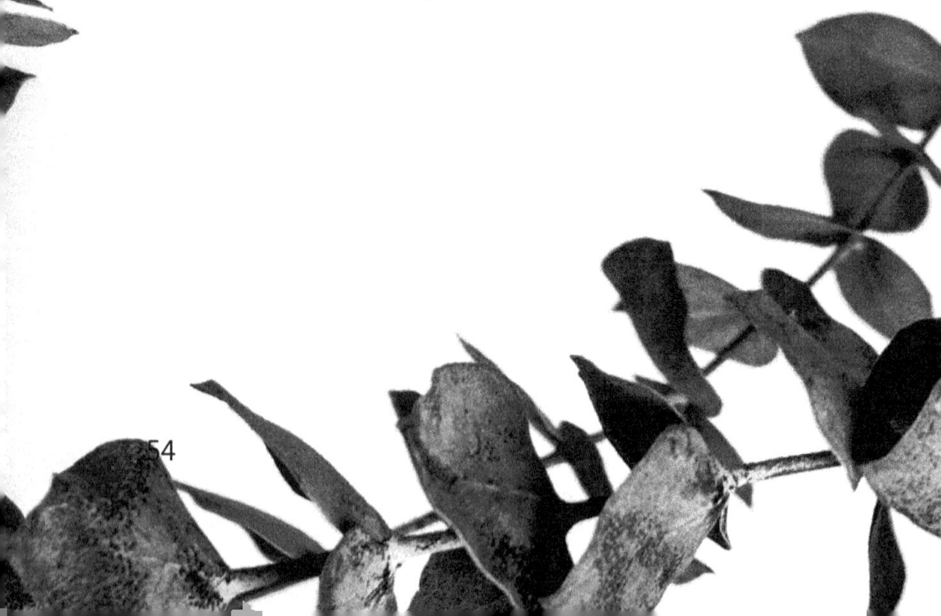

Perhaps when someone asks how old I am
I will say late September or early fall
green still with hints of brazen boldness
showy flare and promise of a fire
that burns without burning
and collected for the colors of my imagination
pressed between sheets of waxed paper
sealed shut with an iron preserving eternal flame
keenly aware of the inevitable dropping of leaves
to be raked into piles for childlike pillow jumping.
I imagine in a world of seasons
less women would pretend to be evergreens
there would be more rosebushes and climbing ivy
boasting of the fruits and blossoms born
boldly celebrated deep roots and expanses climbed.

/the weight of it all/

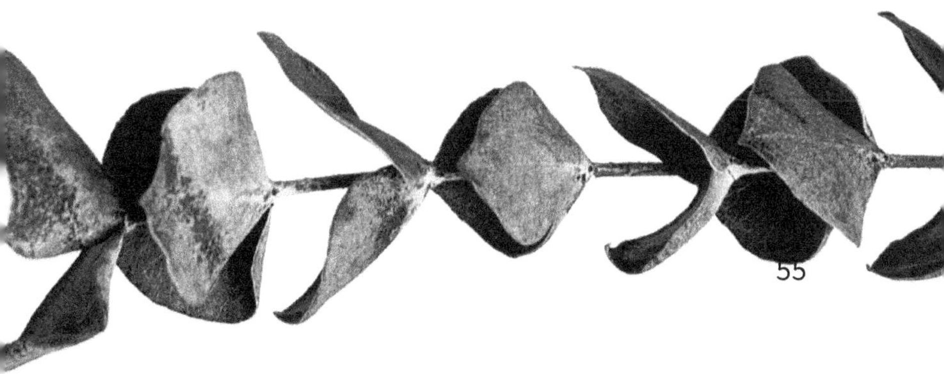

She’s so much darker than I can understand
picking up dead butterflies and bones
as souvenirs to bring home
and I want to learn everything
she was born knowing.

/pisces/

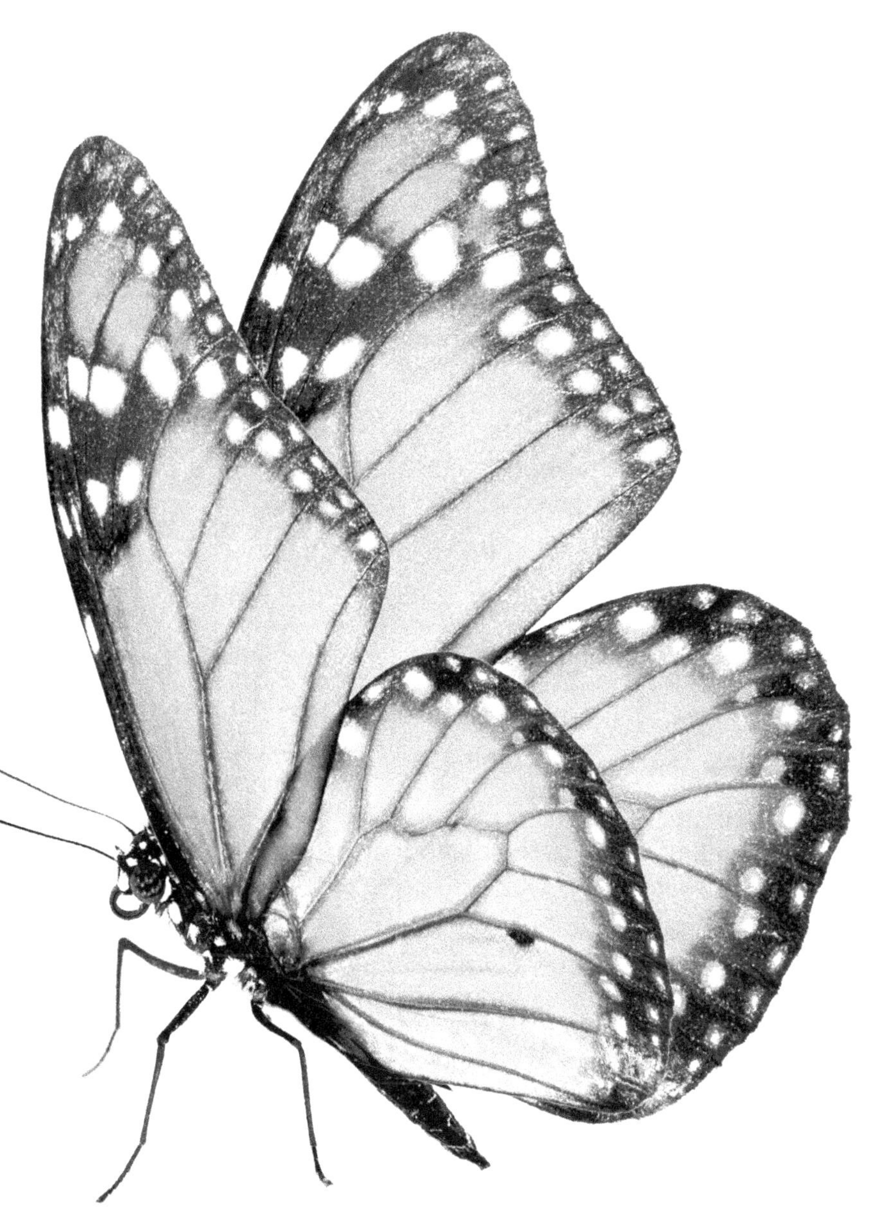

I will offer you my gatherings
of dried flowers preserved in frost
and you'll remember beautiful stories
of their once was
after the fragrance and vibrance
has left their stems dry
their form and persistence
to exist and remain
long after sap ceases.
We find comforting magic
in those martian petals
and symmetrical pods
with dangerously sharp edges
beautifully violent.
Come love, bring me childhood scars
let me count them
and listen to the origin
of their birthplace
noticing each retelling
holds a new blossom of detail
like the smell of a fireplace
as you pedaled into the disappearing day.

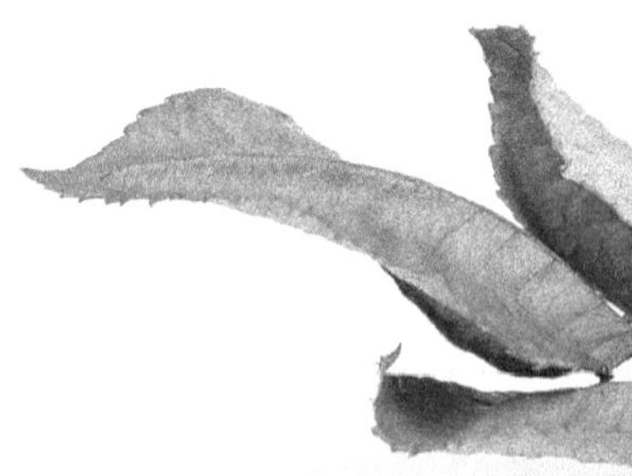

Come love, bring me your shame
the stories you won't ever tell
and I will arrange you brand new
because it's your birth day
each rising of the dawn
full of potential bloom.
Come love, bring me your regrets
and I will assure you
it could be no other way
the years spent wasting
trying to prove you are worthy
or pretty
or normal
because you sometimes worry you're not normal.
And we'll laugh and say
what's normal anyway
but a bunch of ordinary characters
in a book we'd never read.

/wedding day bouquet/

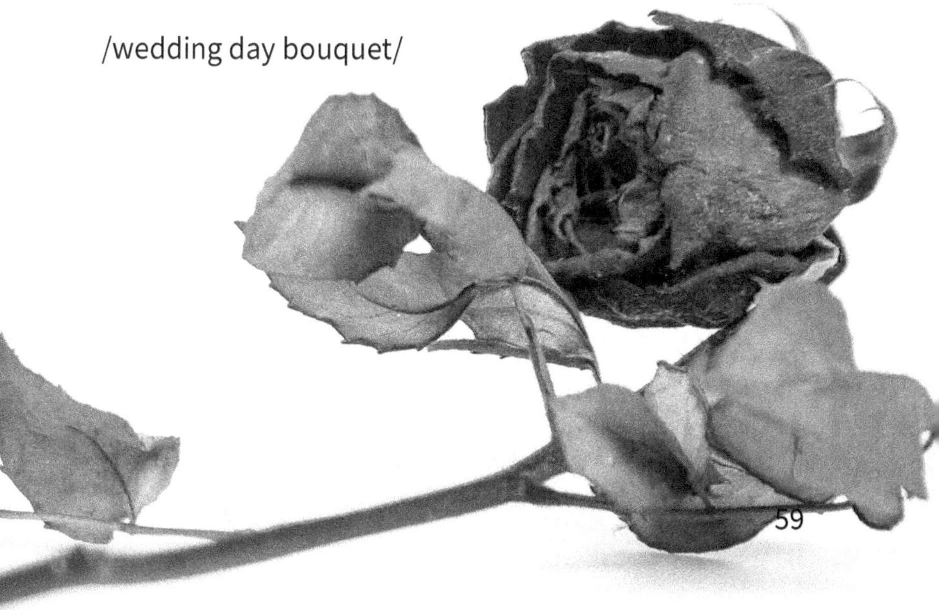

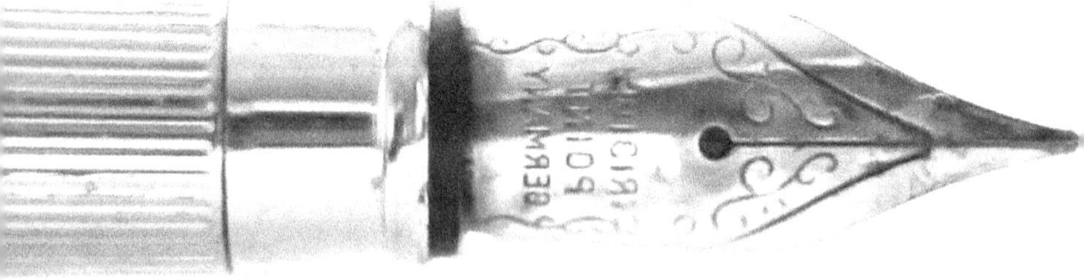

Maybe you're blinded, little miss sunshine
because these blues and bruises are real
and somehow all this will end,
I'll say even though you left me
you still won't leave me in peace
so I get out of bed
or get out of town
and I can't get you out of my head,
because it's you I play on repeat
my favorite drug of choice.
I'm addicted to so many things
I don't know what to quit first
definitely not procrastination
as I'm playing pretend
in a grown up body
as it dissolves around me
pushing off the ending
because I promised you I'd be your pen
if you ever had a goodbye to send.

/your pen/

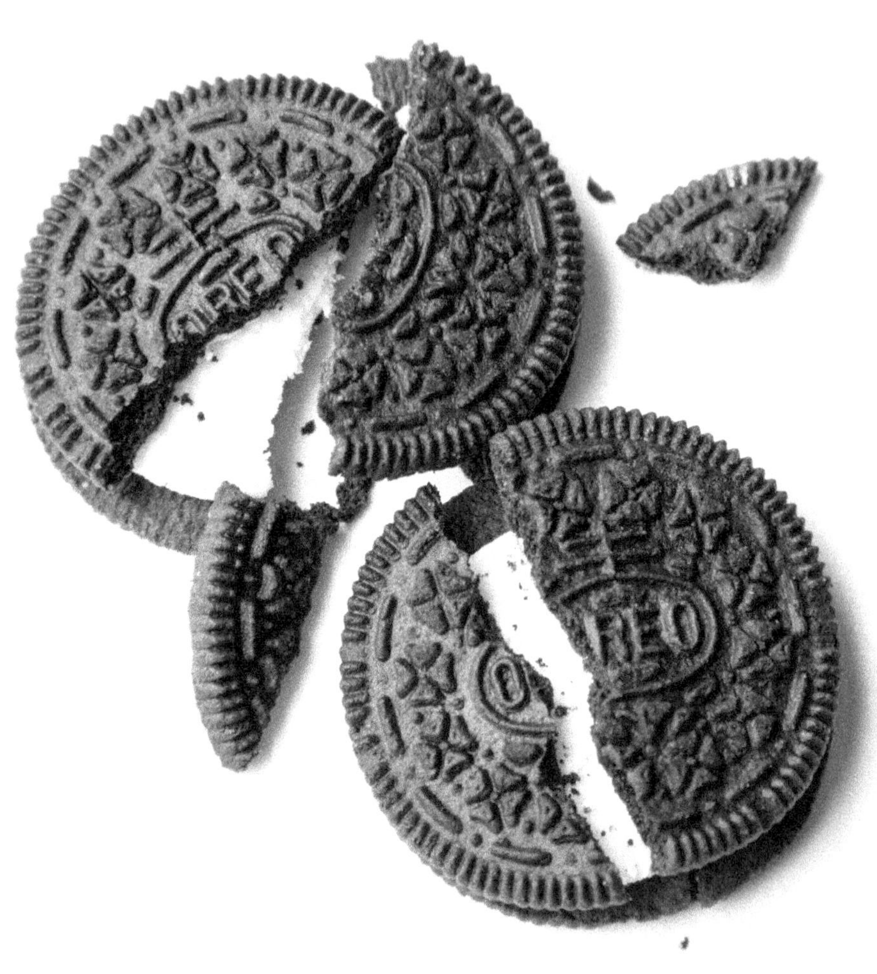

You're temptingly good
you're Girl Scout Cookie good
only comes once a fucking year good
you're a Samoa
a Thin Mint,
if you're not, admit it
say you're an Oreo
anyone can get one of you
anytime they want
no waiting a year for cookie time
you know, no one stashes thin Oreos
in the back of their freezer,
No, you're the REAL good
that's what I'm talking about
the kind of sweetness
I don't want anyone else to have
so I keep it on the down low
I devour you in the middle of the night
under the covers
no guilt
all mine
I waited
now I get to savor every bite,
That's you
you're Girl Scout Cookie good
and I'm hungry.

/girl scout cookie/

Let me not forget
that I contain all the darkest secrets
of the witches who burned before me
who shrank back from your lashes
cowering like a lamb at slaughter
like a house crumbling
under false foundation.
No, I will not cover my shadow
with incandescent yellow insecurities
I engulf you in my velvet rippling
out me, through me, of me
powerful expanding past the heavens
I am the footprints of Gaia
the soot fertilizing earth
and marrow, dark inky insides
I am not made of the stars
it is me that the stars rest within
I am the night sky
the mother creator of all that is light
and without me there can be no shine.

/yin /

My words have cut
leaving red mark reminders
from a careless flick
a hot poker tongue
I swung at that party
two drinks in
and I didn't even remember
but you did
rubbing that scar
a child's skinned knee
I took that virgin skin
and if I knew
I'd lay with you
and make peace
everyday
I'd hand you the brand
burn me
I'll bite off my tongue
to stifle harsh words
but your scar remains
and I'm hostage to those stumbles
with the hands of a giver
and the tongue of a sinner.

/one word scar/

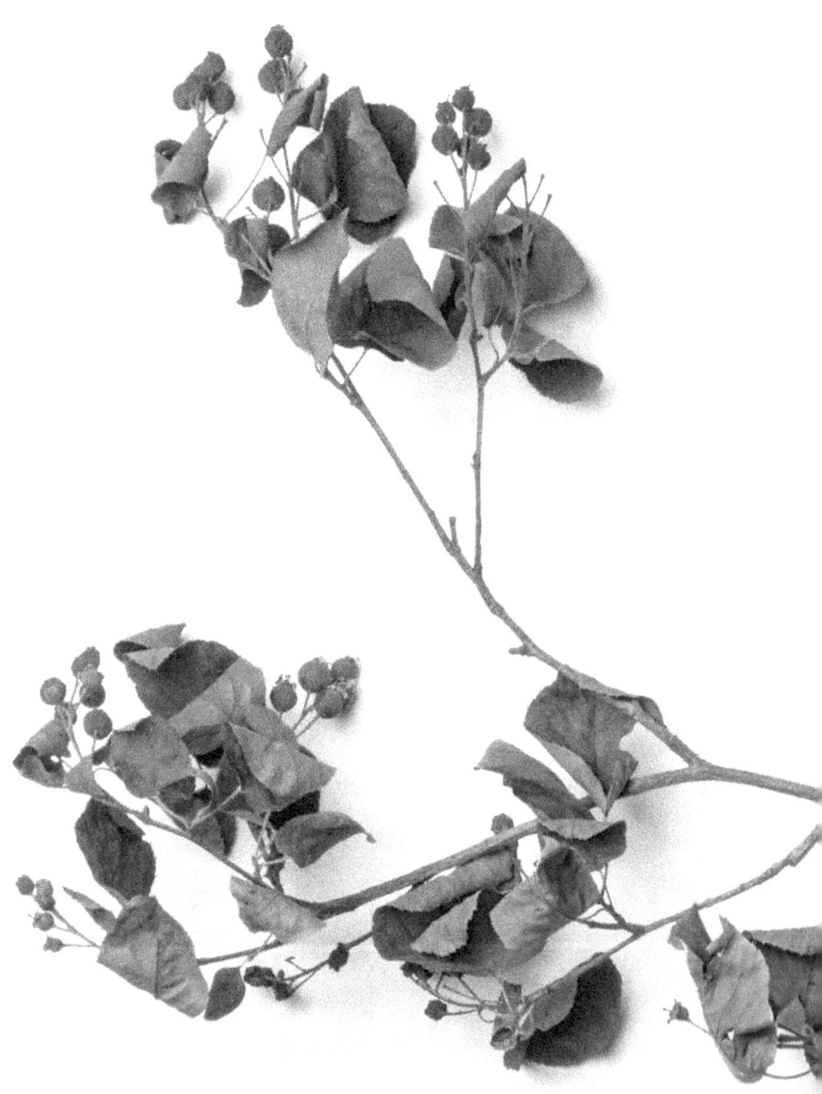

Goodbye to the summer of
pressed flowers
bruised knees
hotel keys
crumbs in my bed
wearing my ring
and playing at love,
I'd say I miss her being mine
she reminds me she never was
a tramp and I'm a stray
looking over each other's shoulders
for a home to find
when we could have been
building it together.

/summertime/

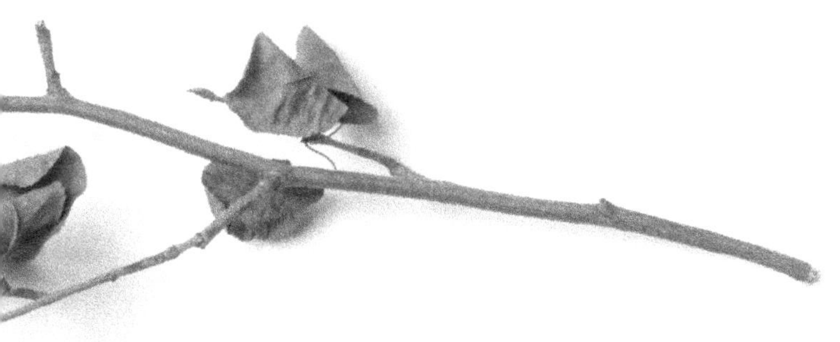

You're moving onto someone else
who makes you unhappy
with your story of shame
as you say your peace
I'm waiting for you
to run out of steam
knowing I'm not this story
you tell others about me
nor the sum of all your stories
like mere words could embody
any one human's magic
and conclude a jury conviction
through old love's filter
of a voyeur's snapshot.
And here comes the blame
raining from snarled lips
I make you feel worthless
stupid and small
I make you feel
less than
feel dirty,
I make you
hurt.
What a Gemini contrast to yesterday
when I made you feel
like the most beautiful woman alive
like anything is possible,
And the sobering truth
I can't make you any of those things
because if I could

I would make you a fly on the wall
so you could see me multiplied
as I go back to the pictures of us
that night we slow-danced in the street,
I'd make you hear the sound of your laugh
through my ears
like church bells to a christian Sunday,
I'd make you remember the thousand times
I told you how beautiful you are,
I'd make you feel my hand
on the small of your back
or running through your baby hair,
I'd make you remember
how I love the smell of you
after working in the sun,
I would make you love me
with all my darkness,
I would make you new,
I would make you mine,
but I can't make you happy
because happiness is a choice
so I will choose for both of us
and make you walk away.

/gemini/

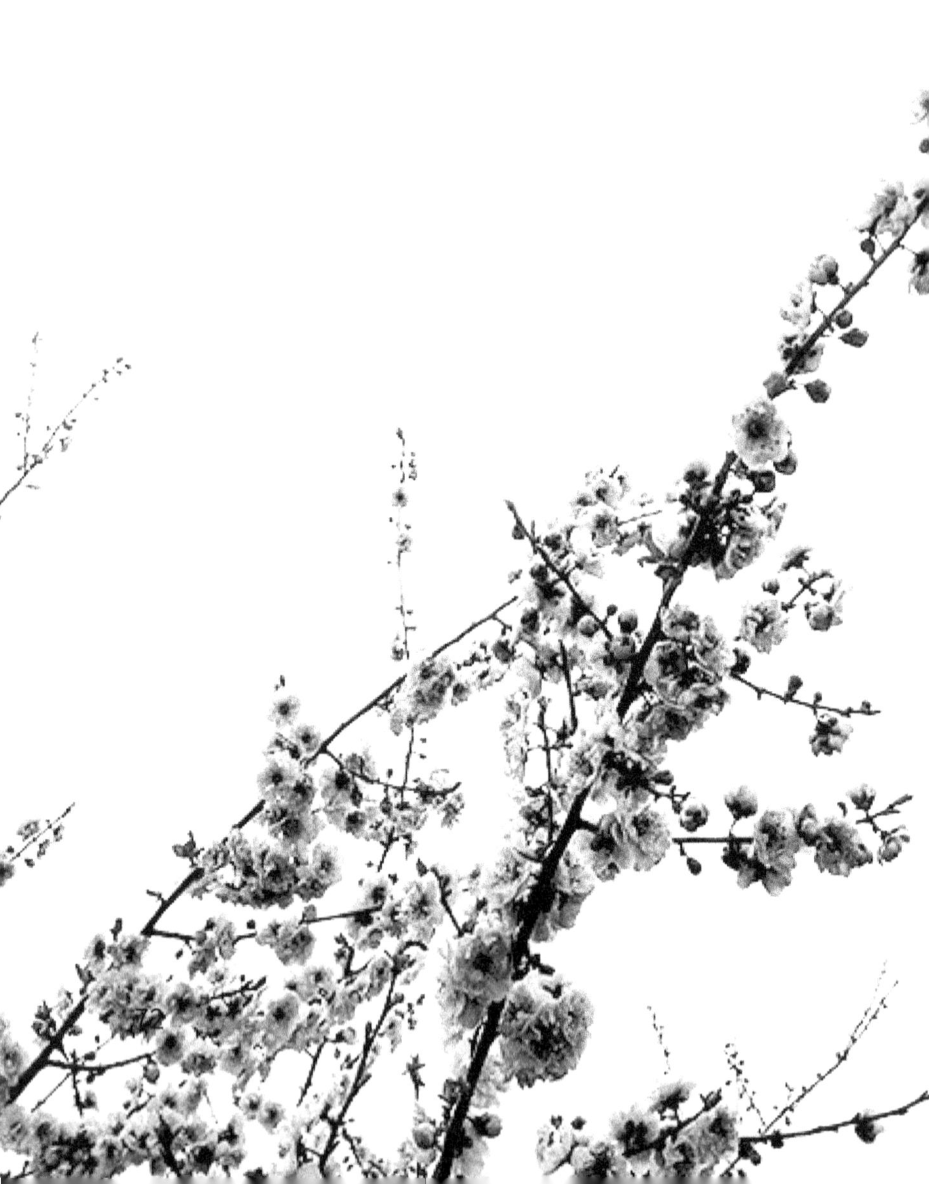

I choose this human
with a past
as perfect and whole
to stand by
with grace and forgiveness
in darkness and in light
through the bleakness of winter
as the blossoming of spring
to honor in loyalty
committed each day
returning to innocence
in this lifetime and all others,
I Do.

/vows/

I wish
our love
to be worn like
small silver rings
with tall tales
that grow grander
like a fisherman
the more I tell
our story
the bigger the fish
that got away.

/catch and release/

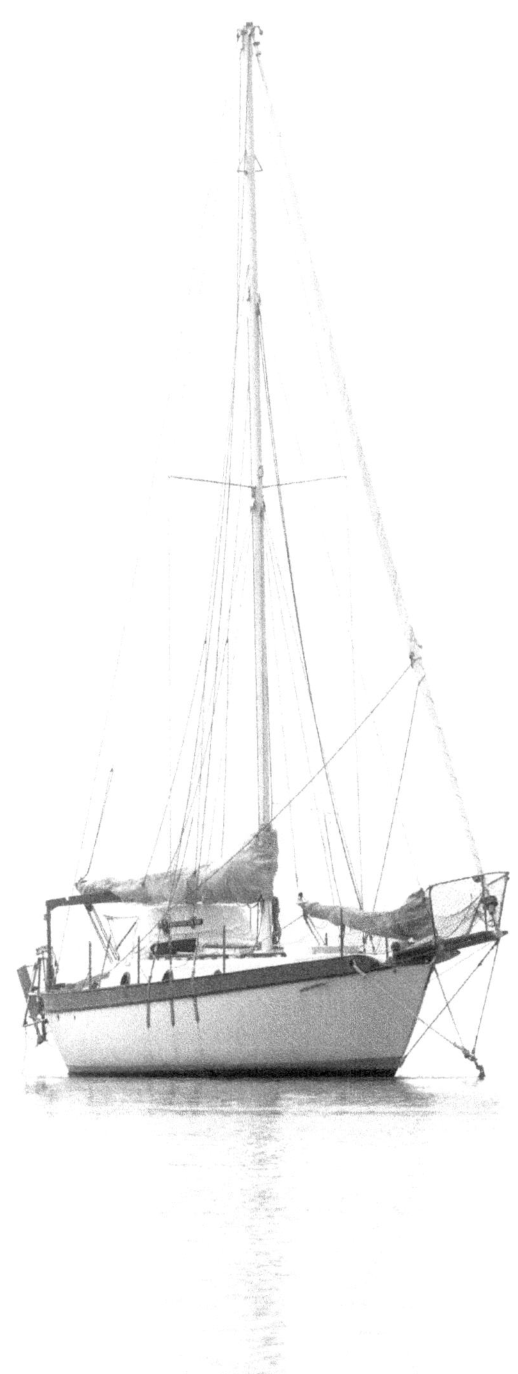

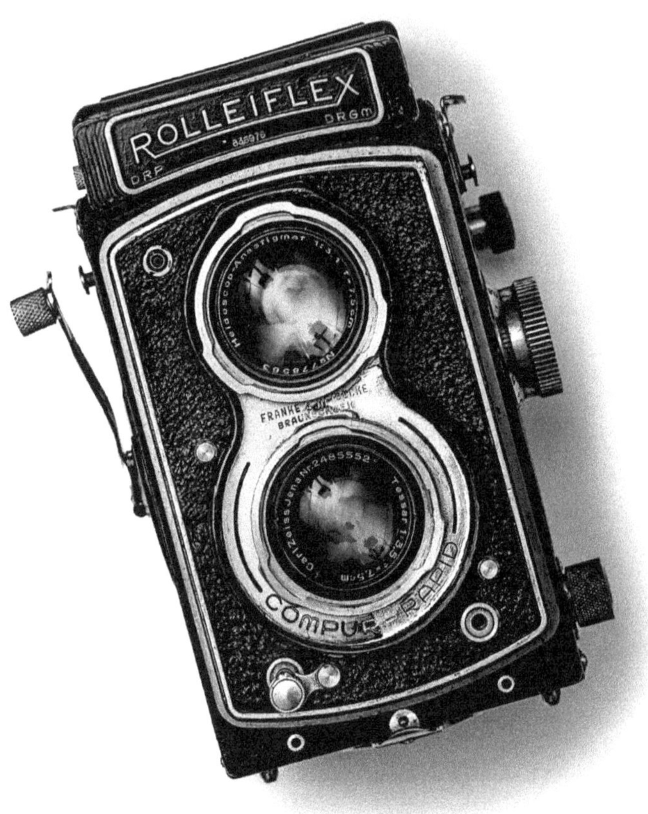
ROLLEIFLEX
DRP
DRGM

Your fucked up
is not nearly as bad
as my fucked up
because I've learned to
keep mine down
and sit stone-faced,
I either decide to let it go
or hold it in,
You're fucked up
keeps leaking out
onto the carpet
and that's unacceptable
in a world of selfies
with friends and followers
counting numbers of likes,
But please don't ever tame it
because I really heart
your fucked up profile
the one you don't post
and wear inside the house
when it's too bright outside
to don a smiling filter,
I'll block those sunbeams
unfriend the sun
and silence the news feed
running through your mind.

/selfie/

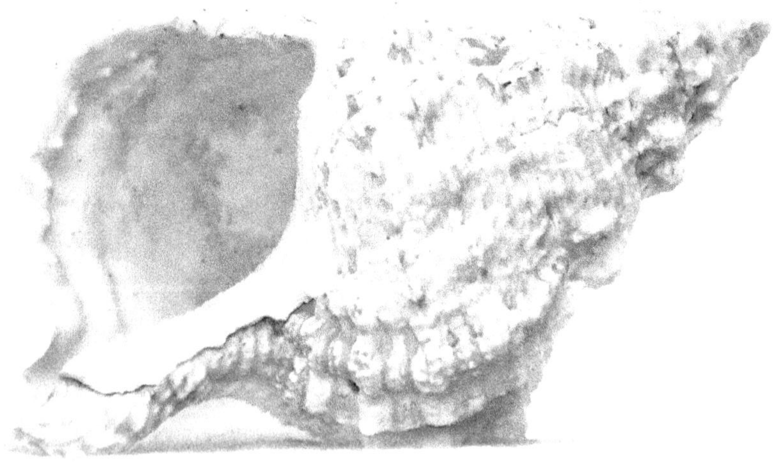

I suppose we are drawn to the sea
the same way we are drawn to the moon
with the pull of water that makes us who we are,
I like to think there's more to the story
that it's the salt in the waves
and our tears that tie us,
lovers and dreamers are drawn to the ocean
with our brokenness
and we collect the shells that are whole.

/seashells/

Books from Tanya Stone:

Call Me Crazy - Poetry and Fine Art Photography
(2019 - Published by Stone, Inc.)

Eve - Poetry and Fine Art Photography
(2020 - Published by Stone, Inc.)

Tanya Stone (born April 24, 1975) is an author, photographer, artist, and poet. She holds BA/BS degrees from University of Massachusetts, as well as an MBA from Florida Atlantic University for Business and Marketing. Although expressing an affinity for art and writing since childhood, she worked multiple corporate careers, including a 17-year career in Information Technology. She formed her first corporation in her early thirties, and later formed Stone, Inc., the umbrella corporation, which includes a clothing line, Tanya Stone Studios for her photography, and the recent Bee and Stone design agency. She is self-taught in fine-art photography, specializing in self portraiture and digital composite art, and refers to herself as a "storyteller," using multiple means of expression as a medium. She enjoys her well-rounded life as an avid traveller, surfer, entrepreneur, and creator of clothing brand Extra Dressing.

Tanya was born in New England and later moved to South Florida, where she resides today with her daughter and fiancé.

www.ingramcontent.com/pod-product-compliance
Lightning Source LLC
LaVergne TN
LVHW020655100826
845148LV00012B/2512

* 9 7 8 1 7 3 3 3 3 4 4 1 9 *